Blessings in Disguise

Carolina Christian Writers Conference

& Florida Christian Writers Conference

Compiled by

Living Parables of Central Florida

Blessings in Disguise

Volume 1

ISBN: 978-1-945976-41-4

Published by EA Books Publishing a division of
Living Parables of Central Florida, Inc. a 501c3
EABooksPublishing.com

Living Parables of Central Florida, a 501c3

Living Parables of Central Florida Living Parables of Central Florida, Inc., of which EABooks Publishing is a division, offers publishing contests at Christian conferences to provide opportunities for unpublished authors to be discovered and earn publishing credits. We publish high quality, self-published books that bring glory and honor to God's Kingdom.

Blessings often come disguised in hard times, difficult circumstances, broken relationships, or shattered dreams. Sometimes the blessings are unexpected hugs from God. The Bible promises us that He will turn all things for good for those who love the Lord. This is the hope believers cling to when the storm clouds gather and when the rain is so hard, we can't see the next step. May you hear the hope these stories bring and are encouraged to look for your own blessings in disguise.

ACKNOWLEDGMENTS

We'd like to thank the directors of our conferences–Eva Marie Everson, Linda Gilden, and Mark Hancock—for encouraging and equipping writers and speakers for the glory of the Kingdom of God. We wish to thank Cheri Cowell and her wonderful team at EABooks Publishing for giving us this opportunity. We thank our many friends and family for supporting us in our writing dreams. And most importantly, we want to thank our Lord and Savior Jesus Christ for His gifts—may this book bring you the honor and glory you deserve.

TABLE OF CONTENTS

Florida Christian Writers Conference

Carolina Christian Writers Conference

El Shaddai – The God Who Really Sees

Sherry Beason-Schmitt

It was a terrible, horrible, no good, very bad day. In a parking lot, off I-64, somewhere in the middle of Kentucky, I stared at my cell phone as wrenching sobs forced themselves, unbidden, from the depths of my soul. Nobody wanted me.

A moment earlier, a short chat with one of my children left no doubts in my mind. According to them I "spoiled their fun" with my religious beliefs that stood in opposition to their partying ways. They told me in no uncertain terms it would be better if I moved somewhere a few hours away where they could come visit when it was convenient.

I was divorced. There wasn't anyone – other than the Lord – to reassure me that everything would be ok. I had no job, no money, and now, no place to live.

When the sobs subsided, I went before the One who has never let me down.

"Where do I go, Lord?" I asked. "What do I do?"

As I waited in the silence, a clear thought quietly came to my mind–Pigeon Forge, Tennessee. I started my minivan and headed to the heart of the Smoky Mountains.

It was the middle of October and traffic was backed up for about a mile onto I-40, as I tried to exit at State Route 66 in Sevierville.

That Thursday afternoon the bumper-to-bumper traffic moved at a snail's pace. It seemed likely there was an accident further up the road to cause such back-up, when in actuality the traffic was comprised of tourists who were eager to see the beautiful mountains and visit the many attractions in the area.

About half-way through Sevierville I pulled into a parking lot just in time for my minivan to run out of gas. Well, this was it. No job, no money, no gas, no place to live. I had hit bottom—God was going to have to do something because I was helpless.

It was a chilly and restless night in my van and the morning couldn't have arrived soon enough.

Rising early, I set out on foot to look for work. The Lord graciously provided a job at the local Shoney's and I was to start the next day.

There was a church right beside the parking lot where my minivan was parked. Inside I asked if there was a way to borrow money until I got paid. They graciously refused the loan and offered a gift instead. They would pay for the first week of a rental room.

Fortunately, the tips earned at Shoney's offered immediate cash, so things began to look up.

What a Lord! Within 24 hours of arriving, He had provided a job, a place to live, food and gas money.

Although the pay for the serving job at Shoney's was decent, I wanted more of an established job, preferably in the area of graphic design. Someone suggested that I apply at a small newspaper, The Seymour Herald, in the next town over.

The publisher, Joe Karl, led me into a small conference room with a large table, surrounded by office chairs. A black laptop was the only item on the table. Karl sat down in front of the laptop and offered me the seat to his right.

A man known for his zest for life, as well as a seasoned reporter, Karl began to rapidly ask questions.

"Have you ever worked for a paper before?" "Have you ever been to county or city meetings?"

Fortunately, I grew up in a family that was very active in local, as well as national government, so I was somewhat familiar with what happened in those arenas.

His piercing eyes seemed to search my face as I worked to respond to his questions in a satisfactory manner.

Finally, a question that totally blew my mind.

"I don't need a graphic designer, can you write?"

"Well," I stammered, "I did well in college English."

As we talked, Karl had been doing something on the laptop. Suddenly, he flipped it towards me and said, "Ok, you have just been to a county meeting–write it up."

He got up and left the room.

I sat there stunned.

Feeling as if things were a bit surreal, I began to type. The imaginary county meeting was about a real controversy in the area– he serving of liquor.

When Karl returned, he slowly read the article, then looked at me with a puzzled look on his face.

"Have you done this before?"

"No."

"Well, let me think about this," he said. "Thanks for coming by."

Days of job hunting yielded one offer, so I accepted a job that I thought was selling real estate. It turned out to be a time-share doing telemarketing. I was devastated. Apologetically, I left at noon. I had quit the serving job, so here I was again with no job.

"Oh Lord, I have no one but You," I cried, as the minivan sped down the road. "What am I going to do now?"

Quietly, the Holy Spirit brought The Seymour Herald to mind. I turned onto Chapman Highway towards Seymour.

My heart beating, I entered the lobby of the newspaper. Joe Karl was standing at the front counter with his back to me. He turned and gave me a big smile.

3

"I just tried to call you," he said. "Can you start work right now?"

Thus began 10 years of adventure as a newspaper reporter. During those times, I wrote for *The Seymour Herald*, *The Tennessee Star Journal*, *The Apopka Chief*, and *The Jasper County Sun Times*, as well as others in a freelance capacity.

The God of the Universe – El Shaddai – has graciously led all the way. He really is the Almighty One who truly sees. If we cry out to Him, He does hear and answer. He knows how to turn bad things and tough times into blessings in disguise.

Sherry Beason-Schmitt (formerly Sherry Brunson) is a retired newspaper reporter who lives in Mauldin, SC. She enjoys music, hiking, computers and reading.

The Garden

Michelle Viscuse

He started knocking. It was a gentle, consistent tap, and I almost missed it because I was busy cleaning again. I saw his shadow on the porch as I was pulling back the curtains. The door opened, and he greeted me with a big grin and a long hug. I was really looking forward to our visit.

I was excited to show him all of my progress. The house was clean. There were lists that were checked off every day and each check made it all seem better. The chores kept me busy, and they also kept me focused. He understood it was hard for me to be quiet and still. I believed he wanted me to work hard and do everything "just right." He followed me as I showed him my work, but he didn't seem too impressed.

His focus was on the tightly drawn drapes that covered the boarded-up windows along the back of the house. I tried to pull his gaze away as he made his way to the door that was nailed shut.

As he started to remove each nail, I became agitated.

He smiled and he gently said, "I'd like to show you the garden."

My heart began to race because I knew there was no garden behind that door. I sealed that door long ago hoping it would never be opened again. I worked hard to make him proud and yet none of those efforts seemed to matter to him. **He wanted to open that door.**

5

It took some prying, but eventually, it opened. The smell alone wrecked me. An aroma of death and decay permeated my entire being and made me feel faint. It was very dark. I begged him to shut the door, but it was clear He wanted to be in the awful place that he kept calling the garden.

He had his big flashlight and as he pointed it towards the debris, he asked me to follow him. As we moved, he could tell it was incredibly hard for me. We dug into the soil to remove the heavy rocks. I felt the cuts from the tiny shards of glass and barbed wire. He carefully tended each wound as I cried.

There were tall walls blocking the sun. We pounded away with sledgehammers and eventually they all fell. When we were finished removing all of the debris, I was tired and thirsty. He offered me a drink. I don't remember water tasting so good and refreshing.

Light poured into the darkness.

After a brief rest, we grabbed shovels and rakes and started to work the hard and dry ground. At times, I longed to be back on the front porch, smiling, waving and pretending all was well.

We were making progress. I couldn't quite see the garden, but I believed he would show it to me.

He brought in healthy soil and started to plant new seeds. I followed along and watched carefully. Some places required water and others needed more light. He knew precisely which seeds to plant where.

He taught me how to find the weeds and remove them before things got out of hand.

He repaired the door and it looked shiny and new. I looked forward to walking through it each day to see the progress. For a while, it still looked like an empty field awaiting a harvest.

Then one day there was a bloom, and then another. Slowly but surely there were trees, colorful plants, fruits, and vines. We added bird feeders, butterfly bushes, hammocks and a small gazebo for shelter in the rain. The once dark and dreary place was transformed into the most luxurious garden and it was now my favorite place.

Finally, I asked him how he knew about the garden.

He explained that he actually designed it long ago. He took great care in planning every detail of the home, including picking the best lot. He wasn't just a gardener after all. He was the architect, the builder, and the original owner too.

When I asked Him why he destroyed it, he looked at me shocked! He said, "I would never destroy my masterpiece. Why would I destroy my very own design?"

With tears in his eyes, he shared in vivid details, how thieves broke in and plundered the back of the home when they thought no one was looking. They soiled it and continued to dump piles of devastation onto the mounds of debris. He knew everything.

I cried when I saw how angry and hurt he was because I understood. I had lived with that stench for a long time and had tried everything to hide it.

I asked him why he came back, and he spat as he spoke through clenched teeth, "I never left. I was here for every moment of the destruction. I saw it all."

I still was confused, so I asked him, "Why me? Why now? Why did you rebuild the garden with me? I don't understand."

Patiently, he drew me close and looked into my eyes. He said, "Every home I design has a gar-den. Tell them to invite me in and allow me to pry open the doors that have been sealed shut. Yes, the work is hard and there will be tears, but a beautiful and healthy garden awaits them too. Show them I am worth it."

I looked into His eyes and said, "Yes, Lord. I will."

Michelle Viscuse courageously shares her story of healing in order to inspire women who have been sexually abused or violated to find courage, hope, and freedom in Jesus Christ. Visit her blog at http://www.journeypink.com and connect with her on social media @michelleviscuse.

He Is

Tracie L. Alston

He is my beginning and my end
He is my trust, and my dearest friend
He is my joy and my sorrow
He is my hope for tomorrow
He is my provider in the midst of storms
He is my protector from all harms
He is my comforter in my tears
He is my guard for all of my fears
He is my lover when I need love
He is my shepherd from above
He is my healer in the time of pain
He is my leader, as I call his name
He is my money when I am poor
He is my always open door
He is my judge when I need grace
He is my feet, as I run this race
He is my heart full of dreams
He is my shoulder where I need to lean
He is my understanding when I'm confused
He is my hand holder, when I'm misused
He is my faith when hope arise
He is my Blessing in Disguise
He is my Lord, that was sacrificed
He is my Savior, Jesus Christ

Tracie L. Alston is a native from Raleigh, NC. She has a Bachelor of Arts degree from Winston-Salem State University, and a Master of Divinity from Campbell University. She has started the organization Prayer Bridge, INC developed, to encourage Christians to connect to God in and through prayer. Prayer Bridge, INC's mission is **Connecting Christians through Prayer.**

An Orchestrated Mistake

Lynne S. Head

It had been a long time since I had seen my friend Cindy. We met for lunch at her family- owned Mexican restaurant in a little town in western North Carolina.

I anticipated our time would be wrought with emotions. Years before, our sons had played together on a soccer team in middle school. Now her son was in college and my son was in heaven. We reminisced about our sons' friendship and about my son Andrew's tragic death seven years before. An all-too-familiar anguish splintered my heart as we wept, but joy mingled with my aching as I heard how Andrew's life had caused a classmate to turn away from a destructive habit. My heart calmed to a steady rhythm as I rested in God's purpose for Andrew's life.

As we talked about trusting the Lord for having His hand in all things, big and small, Cindy shared a story about how God will take even the smallest thing as a misdialed number to bring on a huge blessing.

"Last week my daughter, Haley, called me while she was at school. I couldn't answer right away and tried to call her back. A male voice answered her phone and when I asked for Haley, he joked and said he was her husband. I was in a hurry and replied, 'Just have her call her mom.'"

"A few minutes later, I got a phone call from an unknown caller, so I ignored it. A minute after that, I got a text from someone asking why I was calling her husband's phone. I felt embarrassed, realizing I must have dialed a wrong number when I had tried to call Haley."

"I texted back saying I couldn't answer her call because I was busy at work with a customer and apologized for my mistake. I explained that I just thought one of my daughter's friends at school had answered her phone and joked about being her husband." "I wrote, 'It was my bad. Sorry for the trouble.'"

Then Cindy turned her phone toward me so I could see the reply from the unrecognized caller: "I know this may be odd, but I wanted to say thank you for calling my husband's phone, LOL. My name is Haley. I lost my mother this year on February 28, and I just prayed that God would send me a sign of her. I don't know if it is a coincidence that your daughter's number is one number off from my husband's number and that her name is Haley. When I saw your name at the end of the text, I just started crying. My mother's name was Cindy. It brought me so much peace and I just wanted to say thank you."

I looked up at Cindy as my heart swelled in wonder. A smile spread over her face as she declared, "God took my mistake and made it a blessing!"

Lynne Head serves as a licensed professional counselor in North Carolina and works as a counselor for her mission, World Team. She served as a church planter in Paris from 1997-2002. Lynne is writing a book for women who have suffered sexual abuse and shame entitled, *Call Me Daughter*.

Blessings in the Mix

Brenda Culbertson

Joy is contagious, infectious, and spreads quickly. Have you ever considered that resting in Christ may actually involve serving someone else joyfully? As you rest in Christ, He may guide you to share joy by serving another person. Then, while in the process of serving someone you may unintentionally impact someone else's life that you were not expecting as a total surprise. No doubt, your act of kindness may stun a complete stranger. God has a divine way of surprising us and others in the giving away of joy and love.

Not too long ago, I was in the process of moving. The final days before we closed on the house were fast approaching. Being a doer and a recovering perfectionist, I thought that I could do it all without the help of my amazing girlfriends. Each time the calls came I replied the same, "No thank you. I appreciate your checking on us, but we are all good. My husband and I are on target for getting it all packed up on our own." Foolishness! Never turn down the blessing of help from great friends. So, the final day arrived and I was in a state of panic. Honestly, I felt like our stuff kept multiplying. I was still trying to sort, organize, and clean while boxing things up and I was in desperate need of help. Finally, I swallowed my pride and called several of my girlfriends to come help. To the glory of our Heavenly Father, help arrived. My girlfriends quickly put me in my place. It was too late for any tactic of organization. We were in full stress mode and EVERYTHING was to go into boxes.

"Sort it out later," they explained. Now that's a message for another time.

My sweet friend, Mariko, stayed up with me and worked all night. We packed and then drove and delivered stuff to the new apartment. Then we repeated – all night! During one of our trips to unload boxes, Mariko said she needed something to drink so I told her to follow me through the drive thru window at McDonald's and order whatever she wanted and that I would pay for her order. Meanwhile, a truck pulled in between us. I pulled up and placed my order and then added, "I will be paying for the car TWO behind me." I was a little surprised at the cost. I thought she was only ordering a large sweet tea. How could her tea cost that much? But then I realized she must have been hungry, so I just paid for the order without any questioning. I picked up my order and drove ahead to wait for Mariko in the parking lot. A few seconds later, the truck that was directly behind me pulled up and started talking to me through his passenger's side window. I slowly rolled my window down, and to my surprise he thanked me for paying for his dinner. He said that no one had ever done anything like that before in his life and he was so amazed. Then it hit me! The cashier thought I'd said, "I will be paying for the car TOO behind me! Not TWO cars behind me." WHAT?! I knew that Mariko did not have any money with her. Before I could say anything more, the man added, "I was so moved by what you did that I paid for the person behind me. I have never done that before either. Thank you for what you did tonight." And off he drove into the dark night. Mariko pulled around and I laughed so hard as I shared the story with her. I explained to her that when I got the bill, I thought, "Wow, she ordered a lot." In trying to bless my best friend, who was blessing me, God pulled in a complete stranger and multiplied the gifts being offered. I want to encourage you that no matter how small the gift of joy you spread, you can't underestimate the multiplication powers of God.

Today, why not look for a small way to bless someone else. Send an old-fashioned hand written thank you card to someone. Send flowers or pick them and take them to someone. Stop by someone's work place with coffee and a note and leave it on his or her desk. Bake sweets for your neighbors. Offer to watch a friend's child. Bring a meal to someone in need. God will direct you. Ask Him where He wants to spread a little joy today. And look out, you never know who will be blessed in the mix. After all, He is a creative God and He knows how to take our offerings and multiply the gift to maximize the impact of our simple acts of obedience, love and kindness. Trust Him with the outcome. You may be a blessing in disguise.

Brenda Culbertson is a co-founder of SmartGirl Ministries, a non-profit organization that equips young ladies and women with truth about their value in Christ. As an author and speaker, Brenda uses both Scripture alongside stories of God working in her life to connect others to a faithfully pursuing and loving God.

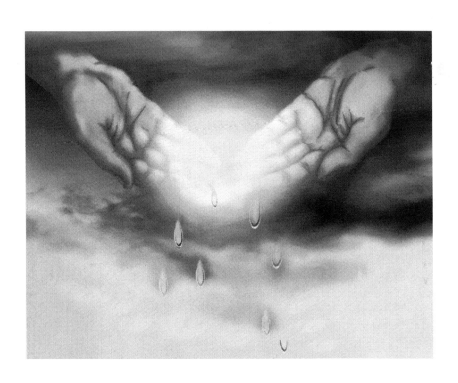

Praying Tears

Kelly Hope

He Somewhere along the way, I planted
Seeds of sorrow and buried them deep;
Watering them with my tears.
Seeds of regret,
Seeds of loss,
Seeds of doubt,
And doubting the heart You gave me.

Deep down in the garden of my heart,
I wondered if any of it could ever be
Healed,
Redeemed,
Restored;
If beauty could somehow rise from my
Scattered hopes and prayers.

So I cried to you, Lord;
You heard, and You came near!
Receiving my praying tears,
Restoring my soul,
And reminding me You are the God
Who blesses empty hands
Raised in surrender to You.

Kelly Hope is the author of thirteen *Keys for Kids* children's devotionals and a poem published in *Teen Quest* magazine. She has also written two plays for the children's church drama team at Forest Hill Church. A former military and missionary kid, Kelly now lives in Fort Mill, South Carolina.

When Rejection is a Blessing

Barbara Harper

Eighth grade was one of the lowest points of my life. Granted, junior high is probably no one's highest point. Changing bodies and hormones, acne, angst, and awareness of the opposite sex all contribute to the awkwardness of that era.

My family moved between my seventh and eighth grades of school. Though I was never a social butterfly like my two younger sisters, I never had trouble making friends. Until then. No one reached out to me. No one responded to me. I spent every lunch hour walking around the campus by myself. My mother had to practically push me out of the car every morning as she dropped me off at school. Finally, one girl had pity on me and sat by me at lunch. She must have noticed I was miserable. But I was too teary-eyed to speak much, and I never saw her again.

Eventually I met another girl who was, for reasons unknown, a social outcast. We became friends for years, and that one friendship was enough to make junior high bearable.

Over time I realized that the school was divided into distinct cliques. Every school or organization has groups with like interests or friendships formed over years. But this school had the most rigid divisions I had ever seen. Interaction between the groups only occurred in small talk in passing, usually only if no one else was around. A few years later when one guy asked me out, several people in his group tried to get me to drop my one main friend. I refused.

She was my friend, my only friend for years. I was not about to drop her!

Before eleventh grade, my family moved again. This time my school was much more hospitable to new students, and I had no trouble fitting in. I still kept in touch with my friend from junior high, Dawn, via letters. We wrote each other through the rest of high school and through most of college, when different interests took us in different directions.

In one of our letter exchanges, Dawn mentioned a young man that I had a crush on years earlier. Brent (not his real name) was in the most popular group. I knew I had no chance at all of ever attracting his attention, much less garnering a date. Dawn told me in her letter that Brent had been involved sexually with another girl from school who became pregnant with his child. There was no love between them. They had just hooked up. I found out later that, in that small town with nothing much else to do, a lot of the teens were hooking up. Others were involved in drinking and drugs.

It was then I realized God's great mercy in keeping me outside the main groups of friends in that school. That had been a vulnerable time in my life. Besides the usual early teenager issues, I was processing the breakup of my family. The move before eleventh grade was necessitated by my parents' divorce. The whole year before their breakup was a highly unstable time in my life, an even lower point than eighth grade. If I had been a part of these other groups, who knows what resources I would have sought to deal with the pain and uncertainty of my life.

Instead, God used my parents' divorce, our subsequent move, and all that pain and confusion to bring me to Himself. I cried out to Him, and He led me to a Christian school, led someone to pay my way when we couldn't afford the tuition, and led me to a good church. I heard the gospel, believed on Jesus, got started reading the Bible, and grew in the Lord. Eventually I went to a Christian college where I met my husband.

Sometimes I look back on that scared and lonely girl I was in eighth grade, and now I'm thankful for the blessing that time of rejection became. God used it to keep me from the wrong path and to prepare my heart for my need of Him.

Sometimes we experience rejection because we're not ready for the opportunity and we need to grow. Sometimes God allows rejection to lovingly steer us away from a harmful path and to a better one. God knows the bigger picture and knows what is ahead.

God was rejected, too. People all through history have told Him "No." In His case, the fault was not on His side. When Jesus came to earth, took a human body, and lived here for over thirty years, He attracted crowds at first. But then people began turning away from Him. Many actively opposed Him. Even His disciples, who were the closest people on earth to Him, forsook Him for a time. But through that rejection, God provided for our salvation through Jesus' death and resurrection. He took what was meant for harm and turned it into the greatest good. Hebrews 4:15 (ESV) tells us, "For we do not have a high priest who is unable to sympathize with our weaknesses, but one who in every respect has been tempted as we are, yet without sin."

Rejection is painful, but when we look to our Savior, He will meet us in our pain and work our circumstances out for the best. He can make rejection a blessing in disguise.

Barbara Harper has 15 years' experience writing newsletters for her church women's group. She wrote a neighborhood newspaper column in high school, has had articles published in four magazines, was a community guest columnist for the Knoxville News Sentinel from October 2011-October 2012. She has maintained a blog with a steadily growing readership for almost 13 years (Stray Thoughts at barbarah.wordpress.com). She has been married for thirty-nine years and has three adult sons, one daughter-in-law, and one adorable grandson. She loves reading, writing, and creating cards for her friends and family.

Finding God's Blessings in the Pain

Nancy Bockstiegel

Sunday, April 2, 2017. This is the day the journey began. That day marked the beginning of a series of events that would forever change my life, my family, and my relationship with God. After receiving a phone call from my brother that my mama had fallen, I raced to the hospital to meet the ambulance. A CT scan and x-rays confirmed the doctors' suspicions; she had broken six ribs and had a punctured lung. She spent thirteen days in the hospital, and I spent thirteen days on an emotional roller coaster, trying to balance work, family, and time with Mama. She later told me that she didn't remember very much about that first week. I knew that was probably for the best.

After being discharged, she continued to heal, and my fears of leaving at the end of May for my family vacation subsided. Little did I know that when I returned, we would be dealt another harsh blow. While I was gone, a small cyst appeared on Mama's right side, the same side she had suffered those broken ribs just two months earlier. We agreed that we would have her doctor look at it the following week during a regularly scheduled visit. The doctor wasn't sure if it was a cyst but decided to refer Mama for an ultrasound. The next day, we heard the dreaded words, "I suspect you may have a fast-growing tumor."

The biopsy revealed that she had cancer, specifically a high-grade sarcoma. We quickly learned that sarcomas are rare, aggressive, and nearly always fatal. From the time she first observed the cyst to the time we received the biopsy results, the tumor had grown from the size of a grape to the size of a golf ball. It was obvious that she had a fight on her hands.

Over the next six months, Mama had twenty-five radiation treatments and aggressive surgery to remove the tumor and as much of the surrounding tissue and bone as possible. Unfortunately, the doctors were not able to remove all of it, so when we met with the oncologist in December, he confirmed there was nothing else they could do. On December 21, Mama entered at-home hospice care.

It was during this time that I began to spend more time in God's Word. I grew up in church but didn't accept Jesus as my Savior until after I had children. Even then, I had a superficial relationship with Him at best. I never had to fully rely on Him. But as we faced this disease, I knew that the chances of Mama surviving were not good. More than that, I knew that I needed strength from God to get through this. I began to set aside time every morning for a devotion and really began to study my Bible. I kept a journal of Bible verses that gave me comfort. I began to truly feel like God was speaking to me at just the right time – a specific verse, a phone call, or a card from a friend. The night before Mama's surgery, one of my best friends gave me a card with this verse: "Praise be to the Lord, my Rock, who trains my hands for war, my fingers for battle" (Psalm 144:1 NIV). I had no idea the battles that we would face in the upcoming months, but I often looked to this verse as I prayed for God to go ahead of me in battle, to prepare me for the war we would fight.

The last few weeks of Mama's life were hard for all of us, especially on days when she seemed confused. It was so hard to watch this strong-willed woman losing the war with cancer. Some days I prayed for God to take her, just so she wouldn't suffer anymore. But he answered my prayer in a different way, in his timing. The day she died, September 16,

2018, she knew the end was near. In a moment of complete clarity, she was able to tell my brothers and me that she loved us. It was her last but best gift to us.

The story doesn't end there. Three months later, on December 23, my brother Donnie died unexpectedly at the age of 55. I had always known that call would come one day – Donnie had never taken care of himself and was consumed by alcohol. There was a lot of family tension because Mama had always taken care of him. It frustrated me, but I knew that he was her son and she loved him unconditionally, so I tried not to judge. I didn't realize it at the time, but two acts of love for Donnie would ultimately take care of my brother James and me as we planned another funeral. First, Mama had life insurance for him – she normally paid it quarterly, but when the last bill arrived, she had paid for a full year. In another gesture that I didn't fully appreciate at the time, she had purchased a burial plot for him, just a few months before she died. It was yet another gift from her, being able to provide for all of us even after her death.

Despite all the grief, I was able to look back on 2018 and realize the blessings I had received. I had nine months with Mama after she entered hospice care; months that taught me to enjoy the little things. We had days that we ate lunch together, days that I was able to physically care for her needs, and days that we just sat and enjoyed each other's company. During this time, I saw Donnie nearly every day, and after Mama died, we continued to rebuild a broken relationship. I learned firsthand that God is in control. Looking back, I can see how God orchestrated so many moments that remind me that His blessings are there; sometimes we just have to look.

Nancy Bockstiegel has been married for 25 years and is Mom to two teenage boys. When she's not working or spending time with family, she enjoys cooking, traveling, and curling up with a book. Her dream is to write a book of the "life lessons" she's shared with her boys.

Alone Not Lonely

C. E. *Harris*

Alone in a golden meadow of joy but not lonely.
The time for rejoicing has come and with it the scaling off of
sounds broken in dust.
She has been called to praise to lift high her voice in
exclamation.
It is not a choice, she must.

Rooted in the soil of her calling, she holds claim to her
election of power and truth.
Embedded in the memories of a Lord who has supplied and
guided her again and again her life is her proof.
And she is sure
And she is green
And she is stretched out wide spreading her layered wings.
Overflowing beyond the brim with the Spirit who has
worked out her pain....
Restored she sings.

To give words where voices are shut.
To grow fruit out of the muck.
To shut lies and overcome hurt.
To step fully in her given majesty and worth.

Stoically aware of her limited time in this space, the
dropping particles of sand leaving this place.
Her mind rests on stirring souls to spiritual awakening.
To a mindful regeneration by way of trinity saturation

She has been pried out dark forests of sadness by His
maternal hands.
She has been soothed by His forgiving love time and time
again.

She has been whispered to in the depths of her soul where
coldness reigned.
She has laughed with her God smiling in the face of weary
stains.

She has curled into His arms a little child in need of her dad.
She has stood on a mountain of pride propelled in knowing
she makes him glad.

She has been surprised by His ways in awe of His patience
silenced by His word moved to action by His actions for
her .
The laying down of Himself the taking of pain so great so
that she might live in full splendor.

Where else can her mind reside where else can she spend her
precious time.
Let her praise in full, let her sing in triumph, join in her
water fall streaming toward the shores of Zion!

She may float alone but she is never lonely hands are
waiting to grasp hers.
Hearts are diving in shedding heavy weights releasing pins.
Before them, stands the one who calls her out to rejoice to
praise to sing to clap to live in fullness again and again
and again.

C. E. Harris is a married homeschooling mother of four residing in Atlanta, Georgia. The first poem she ever wrote was in the fourth grade and poetry has continued to be her favorite source of expression. Her faith is always her guiding source with every word she writes.

Blessings

COUNT THEM ONE BY ONE

Unexpected Signs

Courtney Johnson

"My hearing is getting worse," my mom replied, "so maybe I should go to the class and learn sign language. I might need it one day if I lose the remainder of my hearing." Our church offered an introductory sign language class, and my friend Bethani, who is deaf, agreed to teach it. She invited me to attend, and I convinced two friends, my mom, and my dad to join the weekly class with me for the semester. With Bethani leading us, we all plunged into learning sign language.

During the first class, Bethani taught us how to sign the alphabet, one letter at a time. She carefully checked the hands of each class member to make sure we were holding our fingers correctly. Seated beside her, Mom repeatedly showed me her finger positions for different letters, asking me, "Is this right?" Between classes, Mom practiced with me when we were together. She took notes in class, and she regularly pulled out the information she had scrawled on paper and reviewed it with me.

As weeks of the class continued, we practiced signing letters in sequence to spell different words, and Bethani taught us new signs for common words and phrases. No matter what new material we learned, however, she made us practice the alphabet in every single class, continually checking our fingers for accuracy. During one particular class, Bethani adjusted my mom's fingers on two or three different letters, and later that night Mom said, "I must not be forming the letters very well, but I am trying!" Mom started carrying her sign language class notes in her purse, and any time she had a few free minutes, she used them to practice signing letters, one finger position after another, checking them with me or with her notes to make sure they were correct.

At the end of the class, we all thanked Bethani for teaching us how to use sign language. She told us that of all the signs she taught us, the ones we needed the most were the letters of the alphabet. "If you have those," she said, "you can spell words and communicate anything."

Two weeks after the end of sign language class, we stood in the intensive care unit, staring at the breathing tube draped from my mom's mouth to the computer generating the rise and fall of her lungs. One week prior, Mom had been rushed to the emergency room after being t-boned by an oncoming car. She endured a punctured lung, fifteen fractures, and three surgeries. Because her body needed help with breathing, doctors placed Mom on a ventilator, a machine designed to control airflow into and out of her lungs through a tube into her mouth and down her throat. This tube made it impossible for her to talk. The doctors tried twice to remove the ventilator, but her body was not ready for the transition. For six days, Mom stayed on the ventilator, waiting for the doctors to determine that her body was ready for the tube to be removed.

Meanwhile, Mom became more alert, and she wanted to communicate with us. She could hear everything we said, but she could not talk because of the ventilator. At first, she tried pointing and using her eyes, waiting for us to tell her what we thought she was trying to say. She attempted gestures with her hands, but we struggled to fully understand her wishes. Then, we started noticing the positions of her fingers, deliberate movements and placement of her joints, and we realized that she was forming letters. She was creating the sign language letters of the alphabet, one by one. Due to so much weakness throughout her body, her hands shook as she held them up to form each letter, but she patiently held her fingers in position until we correctly named the letter she was signing.

The more she signed letters, the better and faster she became. Within a day of her signing, we took a notebook and pen into her hospital room so that we could jot down every letter she signed. Once she finished signing all the letters of a word, we then deciphered the letters we had written down and pieced them together to voice the words she intended to spell. Mom used signing to tell us her leg was hurting and needed to be repositioned. She spelled out words for us to communicate to her nurses and doctors. She even used her signing to make jokes, which made us laugh for the first time in days. She used sign language until the ventilator was finally removed and she got the use of her voice back.

Mom took a sign language class so that she could learn how to communicate without her hearing. She expected to use signing one day for this reason. Instead, learning sign language prepared her for the unexpected – the need to communicate without talking. These unexpected signs became her voice, her reward, and our blessing.

Courtney Johnson is a writer by God's grace and for His glory. She has written devotions featured in The Christian Broadcasting Network. She is a licensed occupational therapist and lives with her family in South Carolina.

Every disappointment or misfortune can become a blessing in disguise, for which we should be grateful. But only if the hidden blessing is anticipated, expected and searched for will it be found and recognized as such and the most made of it.

— *Saint Basile*

The Mudslide

Konnie Hall

Our friends, Ron and Paige, own a dude ranch outside Estes Park, Colorado called Wind River. The south facing mountainside is warm and welcoming to all who come to ride horses or enjoy sitting around a campfire roasting marshmallows. Wind River is primarily a family camp, but Ron and Paige set aside certain weeks each summer for special groups. Four weeks are devoted to wounded warriors and injured first time responders. Young women rescued from the horror of human trafficking have the ranch to themselves for two other weeks. One week is devoted to families with handicapped children. God has used Wind River in many peoples' lives to begin or continue the healing process and to restore broken hearts. The horses play a large part of the therapeutic atmosphere, whether campers are petting and grooming them or riding them on quiet mountainside trails.

Wind River also schedules a marriage retreat for one week each summer, and my husband and I eagerly accepted Ron and Paige's invitation to be their guests for that week.

When we arrived at the ranch, the sun was setting in hues of lavender and rose, and the corralled horses were grazing at the base of the mountain. The scene was postcard perfect. When we commented to Ron on the memorable scene, he told the following story.

Several years ago, the Wind River Board members voted to add a zip line to the activities at the dude ranch. After the engineers came and worked out a design for the chosen

35

location, the staff anchored the sky-high ride according to plan. Unfortunately, the zip line didn't pass inspection because of safety concerns. To rectify the situation, a huge, time consuming, and expensive gully had to be dug near the suspended cables.

Because Wind River is a ministry, this development perplexed the staff. Why, when God knew from the beginning that the design would not stand the test of scrutiny, did he not let them build it correctly in the first place? Why did they have to spend thousands for a small valley to "make the zip line safe?"

A year or two later, Colorado experienced one of the rainiest seasons on record, and the weather forecasters warned of possible mudslides in the area. They were right. At the top of Wind River's mountain, the deluge loosened drenched soil and gravity took hold. The rolling mud collected large boulders and snapped hundreds of pine trees as if they were twigs. The air was pungent with the smell of pine, and the sound was horrific. Gaining momentum, the mud barreled down the side of the mountain, getting closer and closer to the zip line. The mudslide came to a sudden end when all that muddy mess rolled straight into that manmade valley, which was just large enough to catch it all.

Guess what was on the other side of the gully? The horse corral, home to every one of the ranch's eighty lively horses. The man-made valley saved those horses from certain death had it not been there.

In God's good providence, the unexpected valley was not merely a perplexing mistake to endure, but providential provision and protection from the Lord. Could this be true of your valley as well?

Konnie is grateful Christ wooed and won her at a tender age. She met Kirk, husband of thirty-two years, while attending seminary at Columbia International University. They own Orchard Lake Campground in Saluda, NC where they minister to campers. Together they homeschooled four children, now grown. Follow Konnie at www.storyscrapbook.blog

God's Beautiful Timing

Joanna Eccles

I get impatient when I have to wait. Proverbs 13:12 says, "Hope deferred makes the heart sick, but when the desire comes, it is a tree of life" (NKJV). Though I want things to happen immediately, God's timing rarely aligns with mine. That doesn't make God idle. Psalm 37:34a says, "Wait on the Lord, and keep His way, and He shall exalt you to inherit the land" (NKJV). While I wait, He works behind the scenes to give me abundant life.

Buying my first place seemed to take forever. My realtor had asked for my "wish list." My top priority was buying a single-family house. I rented a house with other ladies and enjoyed the space inside and distance from my neighbors. I also wanted a brick house with a fireplace. In a land filled with hardwood floors, my heart desired carpet to keep my feet warm in the winter. All of this had to cost within my single income budget. For months, my realtor took me to house after house at the top of my budget. Every one required a complete overhaul. I needed something move-in ready. I am not a handyman.

Exasperated by the search, I nearly quit. As a last-ditch effort, my realtor showed me a townhouse because I couldn't afford what I wanted. The place was too far from my desired zip code, but I admired the tiny yard. Then I saw a friend from Bible study. She said the townhouse next to her was going up for sale. Proverbs 16:9 says, "A man's heart plans his way, but the LORD directs his steps" (NKJV).

Maybe God was redirecting my heart to consider a townhouse.

Within a week I saw the townhouse by my friend that was for sale. It had a brick façade and a fireplace. I was disappointed by the laminate floors downstairs, but the bedrooms were carpeted. My realtor bemoaned the dated kitchen, but the green countertops called my name. It was even an end unit, so only one wall connected to the neighbor's home. Other people had made an offer earlier that day on the place. I prayed at my Bible study after seeing the townhouse and signed papers at Starbucks later that night. I let go of my dream of a single-family house in favor of a townhouse so I wouldn't be house poor. A townhouse would still have space for a roommate, and there was less grass to mow. After the contract was submitted, a bidding war started. Fortunately, my contract was chosen, but the back and forth was exhausting.

Though I'd been in the workforce for a while, the reality of a mortgage made adulthood close in on me. I was about to have D-E-B-T for the first time. Scholarships and student aid had covered my college bills, and I pay off my credit card each month. My realtor tried to persuade me that a mortgage was *good* debt. I was skeptical, but God calmed me down. Philippians 4:19 says, "And my God shall supply all your need according to His riches in glory by Christ Jesus" (NKJV). The Lord reassured me that He would provide for me.

The contract stipulated I had to close before the end of the year. But there was so much paperwork. I gathered so many forms, I began to worry the rain forests might disappear before I'd signed the last sheet. I struggled to complete everything, but submitted the last one before my closing date, December 30.

On my closing day, I went to buy my townhouse, but before I arrived, my realtor called with a grim update. The bank did not have its paperwork together. They needed almost two more weeks before I could close. I pulled over to the side of the road and bawled like a baby. After all my efforts, things weren't working. He reassured me that I would still get the place and wouldn't be penalized because the delay wasn't my fault.

Amazingly, the delay was a blessing in disguise. Unbeknownst to me, a new law provided a large tax credit to first-time home buyers. Because I bought my place the next year, my purchase qualified for the credit. The extra funds helped reimburse my closing costs and new household items. I paid less double rent and delayed taxes too. I recalled the peace God had given me in the midst of my worries about money. God wanted to bless me, but I had to wait.

Ecclesiastes 3:11a says, "He has made everything beautiful in its time" (NKJV). God reminds me that His timing is always perfect, even if it is not my timing. He is never late. Fortunately, my lease went through the end of January, so I still had a place to live. I hosted a painting and pizza party so my new place was ready when I moved. A Starbucks napkin inspired the décor of my beautiful townhouse because I love coffee. My accent walls were a bright spring green like the leaves and my long walls were a deep tan that matched the recycled napkin. Those green walls bring me happy thoughts to this day because of all the love my friends put into painting them.

Now whenever my plans go askew, instead of sobbing in frustration, I wonder what surprises God has in store for me. Not every surprise blessing has been as lucrative as the one with my house, but simply seeking God became the gift. I learned God had "thoughts of peace and not for evil, to give me a future and a hope" (Jeremiah 29:11, NKJV).

God knows the future better than I do. Waiting is less of a chore when I recognize that because God sees what I don't,

He is looking out for my best interests. I can rest in His timing, knowing the end result will be for my good and for God's glory. I pray God shows you His beauty when your plans don't happen when you want. When the time is right, may He shower you with beautiful blessings.

Joanna Eccles founded *Words from the Honeycomb* (www.wordsfromthe honeycomb.com) to encourage people to grow in Christ. She desires to shape culture by addressing truths in relatable ways. Joanna has led Bible studies for fifteen years and completed the year-long C.S. Lewis Fellows Program. She lives in Virginia and loves traveling.

Florida Christian Writers Conference

Double Blessing

by Joanna F. Leonard

Calls from Salty Family Services, our church's ministry to families with at-risk children, usually came with a request for me to do something. My day was already full. As I tapped the screen to answer, I took a deep breath. The service coordinator, Courtney, was bright and brisk as she explained that a single mom of twins needed child care the next day because her regular babysitter was sick, and she was scheduled to work. Would I be able to watch Carries six-month-old twins?

I drew a deep breath. Tomorrow was my thirty-fourth wedding anniversary. I was busy preparing for our son's arrival, plus other holiday errands. I also had a biopsy to work around. My husband and I had planned to spend the day together and end it with a special dinner. I told Courtney I needed to talk to him before I could answer.

As I hung up the phone, my thoughts raced. Infant twins! It had been hard enough managing my two boys born eight years apart. God, do you know how anxious I've been about this biopsy? Lord, this is added stress, yet you know I care about this young woman who is trying hard to provide for her family.

This would totally disrupt our anniversary plans. I told my husband, Lanny, that I would only do this if he agreed. We decided to pray.

I continued to run my errands, praying as I went. There were Christmas packages to mail, medications to pick up for my procedure in a few days, and last-minute gifts to buy.

It was 4:40 pm when I made my last stop of the day. Courtney would be leaving her office at five. Because I'd asked her to continue to call other volunteers, a part of me was disappointed she had not yet let me know she had found someone else. Lanny said it was up to me and I knew God was asking me to meet this need.

I called Courtney, "I honestly can't say we're excited about caring for the twins but we're willing. Courtney's appreciation was more gracious than my acceptance. She told me Carrie would call me to make arrangements.

A few minutes later, Carrie called. We were needed from two in the afternoon till nine in the evening. There went our planned quiet anniversary dinner. I felt a pang, but there would be other anniversaries. I didn't want to miss this opportunity to help a single mom in need.

Then Carrie called back. Her supervisor wanted her to work the day shift instead of the evening. Would we be able to watch the twins from eight until four o'clock? I agreed and we made the arrangements. As I hung up, I lifted my eyes heavenward and whispered, "God, you're amazing. You knew I longed to spend the evening with Lanny, so you rearranged Valerie's work schedule. Thank you."

The twins, Max and Maggie, were beautiful. Their precious, dark brown eyes gazed at Lanny and me as we assisted with their transport into our home. There was formula to mix, diapers to change, and lots of cuddles to give. They were breathtaking. Their smiles and belly laughs stole our hearts. At one point, Maggie was awake and her brother fast asleep, so I put her carrier seat outside Lanny's office where he was playing his guitar. Maggie was smitten.

The memories of twenty-two years ago flooded my soul with joy. Lanny would often play his guitar for our son, Karson, who would fall fast asleep as his daddy worshiped. "Oh God, you are a God of great blessing."

Carrie arrived on schedule to pick up her children. We sat on the couch and she began to share her story. Here was a single mom of twins, who's own mom had died when she was only ten, determined to do what she needed to do to care for her children.

Her eyes lit up as she described the day, she found out she was expecting both a boy and a girl. I listened as she told us a friend of hers was allowing her and the twins to stay temporarily in a converted Florida room. She reflected on her present income. The job she now had would not provide adequately for her children. She shared her hope of finishing training to become a phlebotomist. This dream job would better meet the needs of her family.

When Carrie stated she lacked confidence in further job search, I looked at her and told her she would make a wonderful phlebotomist, if that's what she wanted to do. I affirmed her ability as a mom and told her the diaper bag she had prepared with every possible need the babies could have was testimony to her organization and detail. I pointed out, as a registered nurse, I knew these were very important qualities when working as a phlebotomist.

We helped her get the babies and their supplies safely in her car and hugged. I took a deep breath, watching as they disappeared out of sight.

God gave me a glimpse into His kingdom through this beautiful family. We were created for relationship, first with our Creator and then with each other. It is through relationship that we experience joy. How often have I missed that joy because of busyness or maybe just not feeling qualified or perhaps having my own agenda? "God thank you for slowing my pace and showing me your love and in turn allowing me to love others.

Bio: Separated from her parents at the tender age of seven, Joanna Leonard endured emotional and physical abuse throughout her childhood at a New Hampshire boarding school. She shares her healing journey on her blog, joannaleonardblog.com and prays that God will use her story to strengthen others on their own journey to freedom.

Separated from her parents at the tender age of seven, Joanna Leonard endured emotional and physical abuse throughout her childhood at a New Hampshire boarding school. She shares her healing journey on her blog, joannaleonardblog.com and prays that God will use her story to strengthen others on their own journey to freedom.

God's Timing, Not Ours

Deanna Beaver

Children are a gift from God. They come in all sizes with different traits and problems. Our son was no exception.

Caleb was born on May 3, 1994. He ate well, grew fast, and made boy noises. However, he was constantly getting painful ear infections. When he was seven months old, our pediatrician referred us to an ENT (Ear, Nose, and Throat Doctor). It was December and I informed the ENT that I didn't care if it happened on Christmas Day, I wanted Caleb to have tubes inserted into his eardrums to help alleviate the pain and infections he was experiencing. The doctor laughed and said maybe we could arrange the procedure for another date besides December 25. Yes!

The operation was a success. Problem solved. Tubes were inserted into Caleb's eardrums to allow for drainage and help prevent ear infections. The doctor said they would fall out within a year or two, leaving the holes in the eardrums to heal and close on their own. That is not exactly what happened. The tubes did fall out on their own. But there was a glitch — unlike the right one, the left eardrum never healed. This meant Caleb had to wear an earplug every time he took a bath or went swimming. He grew accustomed to this small handicap.

Caleb's ear must stay dry because water could contribute to another ear infection. Caleb was a happy child and had a high tolerance for pain. If he ever grabbed his ear and cried, we took him directly to the doctor. It was always an ear infection. The prescribed medicine came in liquid form that had to be put in Caleb's ear. My husband and I took turns holding him down while the other parent administered the drops. His screams of pain were hard to endure. We realized the drops were a necessary evil to help heal the infection. I even tried the drops in my ear to be able to empathize a little of what Caleb was experiencing. The drops caused an extremely cold sensation, and it was uncomfortable having to lie on my side long enough to allow the drops to stay in my ear canal.

Joe and I continued to pray for God's healing, but each doctor visit confirmed the hole remained. We committed to living these verses: "In every thing give thanks: for this is the will of God in Christ Jesus concerning you" (1Thessalonians 5:18) and "Giving thanks always for all things unto God and the Father in the name of our Lord Jesus" (Ephesians 5:20).

Our decision to thank God daily for this hole in Caleb's eardrum led to a stronger faith in trusting God. We certainly did not know God's plans or timing but realized that God was in control and we should be thankful in all things.

Whenever Caleb had a recurring ear infection, we were happy for the hole because it acted like the previous tubes and helped the drainage. As the years passed, we continued to pray but not as fervently as earlier. Each visit to the ENT confirmed the hole was still there. The doctor told us Caleb would have to wait until he was eight years old, when his ears matured, before the hole could be patched with a skin graph.

We continued to use the same earplug for three years. That was a blessing since it was expensive for a silicone earplug to be individually molded for Caleb's ear. Of course, as Murphy's Law would have it, we were about to go on a beach vacation in early August of 2000 and lost the earplug. Forty- two dollars every three years wasn't that bad.

In late August of 2000, we met with our Christian Cell Group one Sunday morning. Caleb was six years old and had yet another ear infection. We requested prayer for him and told them some background information. One member suggested we lay hands on Caleb and ask for healing. We agreed and called Caleb to join our adult group upstairs. Having our friends unify with us in laying hands on Caleb and lifting him up to God for healing, was one experience I'll never forget. Yes, his ear infection did heal. We were pleased and thanked God for the healing. But that's not all!

Joe took Caleb to his ENT appointment in October of that same year. The doctor conveyed he did not see a hole. Joe told him to look again, it must be there. The ENT used another instrument to recheck the eardrum. Once again, no hole. The doctor then ordered a special hearing test on the spot. The Tympanometry is a pressure test that pushes air into the ear to detect a perforation. No hole! Joe told him God had answered our prayers. Caleb called me on the way home and said, "God healed my ear!" I said, "Put Daddy on the phone." I wanted to hear the whole story.

Caleb professed this miracle at church, school, and beyond; so did I. As I relayed this blessing to one of my friends, she said, "Isn't it wonderful how God waited to perform this miracle until Caleb was old enough to personally profess His wonders of healing?" This confirmed to us how God's timing is not ours. It is so important to trust Him and not get discouraged. The six-year waiting period in Caleb's life was our blessing in disguise.

Deanna Beaver has an Ed.S degree in Leadership. She is a veteran teacher of thirty-four years and a Master Teacher with Georgia Tech's Inventure Prize. Deanna is a critique partner in Greater Atlanta Writing Group of Word Weavers International. She is a member of Fellowship Bible Church in Roswell, Georgia.

"When you are in troubled and worried and sick at heart
And your plans are upset and your world falls apart,
Remember God's ready and waiting to share
The burden you find much too heavy to bear--
So with faith, "Let Go and Let GOD" lead your way
Into a brighter and less troubled day"

— Helen Steiner Rice

Pots of Provision

Sherri House

The sweet smell of hot guavas hung thick in the air. The clanging sound of a metal spoon scraping the bottom of a metal pot filled my tiny kitchen. Making guava marmalade is a Southern tradition passed from generation to generation in my husband's family.

Many years ago, as a young bride, I was quickly initiated into this Florida Cracker ritual by my husband's grandmother Willie and his elderly Aunt Lucy, both of whom are renown for taking these tiny exotic fruits and transforming them into a sweet sticky substance that hot biscuits eagerly wait to be bathed in.

My husband loves guava marmalade, not only for the taste, but for the pride of family and tradition that comes with the process, so he usually comes alongside me when I am in the kitchen embarking on this summer ritual. Even with both of us taking turns stirring the dark orange concoction, somehow, we scorched the first batch.

Quickly we realized that the culprit for this disaster was our old thin aluminum cooking kettle, so my husband ran out to buy a large heavy stainless-steel pot while I remained at home anticipating our second attempt at marmalade making. We were soon to learn that God would speak directly to our need for financial provision and shower us with His love and perfect timing.

As I stood at the sink, draped in my white apron cutting up the tiny yellow guavas with seedy red flesh, my husband was dutifully studying the various cooking pots at the store and getting distraught at the high cost of good-quality ones. He selected the one he wanted and was waiting in line at the cashier when an elderly lady behind him spoke and told him she had a pot she had never used which was just like the one he was about to purchase. At her invitation, my husband put the store pot back on the shelf and followed this generous lady to her home believing God might be leading him.

Just as she described, her cooking pot was large, of good-quality heavy stainless steel, and in brand new condition.

When he returned home, he triumphantly entered the kitchen with his prize, and as he relayed his story to me, my spirit quickened as I sensed what God was showing us through this unexpected blessing. So often we go before God, providing for ourselves, using our own resources and trying to make things happen, when all along, God is right there, standing beside us, waiting for us to let Him provide. I could almost hear God speak like a loving Father..."go ahead, use your own resources, pay full price if you want, use your own energies and gifts to provide for yourself, but if you will just wait, if you will just listen to my voice and wait for my timing, I will provide for you".

I was so excited about this reminder of God's provision which He had so lovingly put in our path that I had to call all of our now grown children and give testimony to what God had just done. The more I thought on this, the more I realized what disastrous consequences could happen if we jump ahead of God's provisions.

Abraham knew of God's promise to provide a son in his old age, but when He and Sarah ran ahead of God and tried to make things happen for themselves, entire nations and all of history have suffered the consequences, even as we see in today's Middle East headlines.

Maybe a stainless-steel pot has no historical impact or spiritual significance, but God used it to remind us that in our family, and in the generations that follow, if we would heed God's voice and wait on His timing and provision, we will have what we need. We will enjoy knowing God more fully, and we will bring glory to His name and His kingdom.

As I spread the warm and perfectly cooked guava marmalade on my biscuit, I pray," Oh God, you indeed are our provider! Enable us to sense you standing near. Enable us to hear your voice and empower us by your Holy Spirit to wait patiently on you. Forgive us for the times we have run ahead of you and relied on ourselves. Give us eyes to see and ears to hear as your Spirit directs us and provides for us, sometimes unexpectedly! Amen.

Sherri House has been married 46 years and has 3 children and 6 grandchildren. Mentoring others in their personal walk with Christ is her passion. Her in-home tea ministry, mentoring at women's conferences, and devotional writing are ways that Sherri shares the depth and richness that is found in Christ.

"Faith is walking face-first and full-speed into the dark. If we truly knew all the answers in advance as to the meaning of life and the nature of God and the destiny of our souls, our belief would not be a leap of faith and it would not be a courageous act of humanity; it would just be...a prudent insurance policy."

— Elizabeth Gilbert

Aurora's Gift

Hannah Robinson

We destroyed every spindle, burned every spinning wheel, kept the girl in a cottage far away. Never once did we dream there might be a single spindle left in the kingdom. Even if one remained, we kept six miles between our cottage and the nearest city. We protected her, guarding her night and day.

And yet somehow, the day before the spell would have broken, we found her unconscious beside a spindle, her fingertip dripping blood.

Perhaps we knew all along old Shadowmend would have her way. After all, she had nothing to do but sit in a tower and plot Aurora's destruction. She must have expected our resistance when she cast the spell sixteen years ago. And whatever else she might be, she had never been dull. No. That old faerie, the one we all forgot about at the princess' christening, would never fade from memory now. She'd become a legend. The one who outwitted the Six Guardians, who cursed the princess, who broke our hearts.

If only I'd possessed the power to undo the curse! Daily I relived the christening, when the doors of the cathedral opened and she appeared. Shadowmend, hunched under her black cloak, tapping the ground with her withered staff. In a voice quiet as death, she scolded us for neglecting to invite her. Then she cast her curse.

And I, the only one of the Six Guardians who hadn't yet bestowed a gift, had no power to reverse it. I could only lessen its sting, and vow to protect the child.

And I'd failed. We all had. So our darling, the fragile human child who won our hearts, remained doomed to a hundred years of sleep.

Filled with grief, we decided to visit Shadowmend in her tower and entreat her to lift her curse. We prepared to bargain—and if needed, to fight.

Shadowmend's tower hovered like a dark giant, poking above the canopy of the Forest of Duladin. When we flew to the top, we found her windows closed and boarded.

"Shall we break in?" asked Lilliah, Guardian of the Flowers.

All five Guardians turned to me, awaiting my command. I clenched my fingers into fists. The sight of this tower made me want to destroy something, to ruin Shadowmend as she had ruined my heart. But who knew how powerful she had become? Her decades of silence might be only the gathering of a storm. A battle could prove deadly, and I wished to avoid provoking her wrath, if possible.

I fought the urge to draw my wand. "We will knock first."

Lilliah rapped against the boarded window. "Perhaps she doesn't live here anymore."

"Shadowmend would never abandon her tower. She is a snail. This tower is her shell." I pounded the boards. "Shadowmend, open up!"

"Silly children, knocking at a window." Her croaking voice sounded from inside. "Knock at the door, like sensible creatures."

"The door?" LIlliah's forehead wrinkled.

We six circled the tower. There on the other side hung a door, leading out to a three-hundred-foot drop. I'd scarcely touched my fist to it before it swung open, and Shadowmend stood holding the knob, smiling toothlessly. "Haven't forgotten me after all, have you, Meralda? I see you've brought your posse."

I gritted my teeth. "We've come to negotiate, Shadowmend."

"Come in for tea. I saw you coming and put on the kettle." She teetered across the circular room and collapsed into a rocking chair.

I glanced back at the other Guardians. Some of them smirked. This wasn't the mighty enchantress I'd warned them about. This was a derelict old faerie who once held power, and now held only a kettle of tea and a grudge.

Keeping my hand on my wand, I landed inside the tower, and the Guardians followed me. "We've come to see you about Aurora."

Shadowmend rocked in her chair, nodding. "Yes. A lovely girl, isn't she?"

My blood boiled. How dare she speak with indifference? Hatred, I could tolerate. Violence, I could counter. But this cool carelessness, as though she'd cast her spell for fun, chafed my soul.

"You've cursed her!" I burst out. "She's doomed to sleep a hundred years, and longer if a prince doesn't find her!"

"Peace, child." Shadowmend shook her head, showing her gums in another smile. "I had to give her *something*, even though I wasn't invited to the christening."

"Are you still bitter?" I fingered my wand. "How could you expect us to remember you, when you never showed your face? Kingdoms rose and fell, and you kept silent while we guarded the world. Then one princess was born, and you expected an invitation to her christening?"

"You know she's special." Shadowmend wobbled to her feet and stood by the open door, looking out toward the castle. "You know why I wanted to be there. Never has a stronger woman been born. The girl will do great things."

"Then why did you—"

"Where is she?"

Her question didn't catch me off guard so much as the concern in her voice. I hesitated. "In her bedchambers, in the castle."

"Away from people?"

"They keep the door locked, so you can't kill her."

Shadowmend turned to me, her eyes misty. "Why would I kill such a beauty?" She shook her head. "No. A great plague will ravage the land, and many will die. A famine will sweep the country, killing many more. Wars will rage. Nations will fall. But none of it will touch the child."

I caught my breath. Could it be true?

She looked toward the castle again. "And when the time is ripe, Aurora will wake to the kiss of a mighty prince, and will restore peace to the kingdoms." Her voice faded to a whisper. "I knew I would look like a villain. But it had to be so. For Aurora."

I stared at the old faerie, gratitude thawing my heart. "Then… you didn't curse her. You saved her."

Shadowmend lifted her face. "I will always save her."

Ever since she first discovered Narnia, Hannah Robinson has written YA fantasy. Published by Kingdom Pen and Splickety magazines, Hannah has won several awards for her fiction, and was named 2019 Writer of the Year by the Florida Christian Writers Conference.

Christ – My Treasure

Sara C. Alsup

"Christ, in whom are hidden all the treasures of wisdom and knowledge" 1 Colossians 2:3 NET.

When I was a little girl, I made up a simple game and played by myself because my older brother had more interesting things to do than spend time with me. I collected colored glass pieces which I dug up from the dirt. An easy little amusement. But I entertained myself for hours looking at the beauty of broken pieces of cobalt blue, amber, and crimson. I played a game of imagining what had come in the once-important bottles – life-giving medicines or a lady's fragrant perfume? After I carefully washed them with soap and dried them, I placed the pieces of glass inside my precious box for safekeeping. They were important treasures in my childish playtimes.

Such innocence. Such simplicity. I can only wish for the whole world to know Jesus like that, a treasure to be enjoyed with humility, reverence.

Sometimes I set Him aside in favor of other things like baking, reading, social media or watching TV. Ah, then, I remember He is my everything; all the earth revolves around my Mighty God.

If I am a "treasure" in a clay jar on earth (2 Corinthians 4:7 NET), then He is the "TREASURE" with a heavenly purpose. I am conscious that my expressions reflect praise to Him, using words like cherish, prize, adore, worth, importance, captivating, esteem. So my thoughts of Jesus also change when I am worshipping Him. I picture dancing before Him with joy and happiness or worshipping Him with lifted arms. I wonder at His perfect ways, and determine to make His purposes on earth my passion.

When I speak these praise words, joy leaps into my heart, and peace covers me like a calming river. My life takes a new focus. My will and desires give way to Him, while His will rises in importance in my life. This Treasure meets my cares and gives me His promise of faithfulness. I need these assurances to make it through my day. He promises He'll share wisdom when I'm confused and knowledge when I'm perplexed. He is the blessing I didn't recognize I had. As a child I appreciated the small treasurers, but as an adult I find in Jesus my eternal Treasure.

How can you see Jesus as your 'Forever Treasure' today?

My Prayer., "Father, help me to see You as the treasure of my life every day. You give me purpose and importance in all that I do for you."

I love the Bible! As I study, I learn so much more about God and my heart.

I read different kinds of devotions where I can journal, meditate, and personally apply. I desire to reach a wide circle of people with God's Good News. That's the beginning of my love for writing.

Big Red

Sherry Diane Kitts

"Come on over to the tree. It's time to see what's in these fancy Christmas gifts." Rich summoned the family and brought along his camera to record the extravaganza.

He handed me the bulging one, and I pretended not to know its contents.

I teased, "Is this the plush robe I asked for?"

"You'll see." Rich raised his eyebrows. "Go ahead and open it."

He looked over at me like he had a secret, but ever since our first year of marriage, Christmas gifts have ceased to be a surprise. I recalled the time when we'd been married less than a year, and I naively hid Rich's gifts in the back of the closet.

He enjoyed pranks and called me at my office the next day. He thanked me for the slacks he found and asked, "Are they for me?" I could hear a slight chuckle in his question.

"You shouldn't nose around in the closet. It's Christmas." I didn't find his discovery funny, but Rich received great pleasure when he made me fuss.

"I'm just kidding," he said. "I didn't really find anything."

"Oh yeah?" I said. "That's hard to believe," and from that time on, we purchased Christmas gifts per request.

Now years later, I've received a large box that I'm sure contains what I want. I rip off the paper and pull back the tissue. I'm right. It's a robe but there is a surprise – it's red.

Bright red. It's the fluffiest, loudest, shoutin' red robe of all times, and completely out of my color wheel. My favorites are soft blue or seafoam green, and I can't understand his inclination to purchase this red one.

I tried to eke out a smile.

"This is the only one like you described. They didn't have blue or any other color except white, and I knew you wouldn't like that." Rich gave me his puppy dog look.

It would be unkind to disappoint him since he did make the effort. I held up the fire-engine red robe as my thoughts rewound to the Christmas Eve when Rich's father, Jim, opened an unwanted present.

Jim had a boisterous personality, and enjoyed being in the mix of conversations. He liked to banter with his wife regardless the occasion. She thought he needed a new coat, but he said she shouldn't spend the money. Back and forth they tossed one wise crack and then another.

Traditionally, the family gathered in the living room and exchanged gifts on Christmas Eve. When Jim opened the package from his wife, he looked over at her, and immediately tossed it to the floor. "Take it back! I told you not to buy this coat."

She paid no mind to his shenanigans. "Now, Baby..." She stood her ground. "It was on sale."

I didn't want to repeat that Christmas scene so I graciously accepted the robe of red.

"I like it, Rich. It looks warm and soft and the color's a good change." The thick robe hung mid-calf with long sleeves and a rolled collar.

He pursed his lips into a smile and said, "I'm gonna call it Big Red."

A few years later on the eve of December 31, my mother left this earth for her heavenly home. Like the sudden drop of a deep sinkhole, my chest felt hollow. Grief gripped my bones and tears left salty trails down my cheeks. In the nursing home hallway, I could hear people greet each other with "Happy New Year." Outside, the chilly night air penetrated my heart, and I couldn't shake the raw feeling. Not a moment about that night exuded happiness.

After returning home, I headed for the shower. I stood there and let the warm water cascade down my back. I shivered through the steam as a relentless chill hovered across my shoulders, and then spied Big Red over the door hook. After drying, I lifted it and cuddled inside its plushness. I slid my arms into its sleeves, and it hugged me like my mother had many times. The fleecy collar brushed my cheek like her kisses, and gave assurance that we would be okay. I imagined her soft hands and gentle laughter. I shut my eyes and recalled the aroma of her *Youth Dew* perfume.

The New Year arrived cold and remained so throughout January and February. The robe and I became good friends. Its color brought me cheer and warmed my heart when I needed it most. I'm thankful I accepted my husband's sweet gift, and glad I didn't insist on my perfect color.

Fast forward six years to a more joyous, cold night in December. Rich and I trekked through Epcot at Disney World to attend a Christmas musical, and enjoyed the beautiful performance. Exhaustion overtook us as we walked endlessly in and out of the park, and the next morning I felt its effects. My joints ached as I meandered through my daily routine so I decided to relax outside in the backyard sunshine.

Yep, I donned the red robe.

I felt nostalgic and pulled it around me as I stretched out on the chaise. Through the coolness of the day, the sun shone brightly in the robin-egg-blue sky. The quiet breeze tinkled the wind chimes nearby. Honking Sandhill Cranes flew overhead in a haphazard formation while a jet high above them left behind a silent stream. I enjoyed the rejuvenating surroundings and breathed in the crisp air.

Rich came home from work and stepped out onto the lanai.

"Why are you wearing Big Red?"

"I needed a little comfort," I said, "but I'll get dressed for dinner."

As I walked to my closet, I stopped for a moment and gazed in the hallway mirror. Some of the robe's fluffiness had diminished, but its value had extended far beyond my expectations.

God knew exactly what I needed, and He knew it had to be red.

Sherry Diane Kitts is a member of Word Weavers International and creates non-fiction short stories. Her story, "Free Indeed," received the Loyd A. Boldman Memorial Scholarship to the Florida Christian Writers Conference. Sherry writes about navigating life's journey as she reveals her seasons of labor, love, learning, and laughter.

Enlarge Your Circles

Sally Friscea

I plopped onto the squishy sofa as the mental health counselor closed the door behind us. This was my last ditch effort to solve my long term problem with insomnia.

"Sally, what brings you to my office today?" Shelly eased into her glider with matching footstool.

I leaned forward with my arms resting on my legs. I searched my shoes for a way to quickly summarize all of my failed efforts. "After two years of sleep issues, a sleep study showed I woke thirty-three times and slept at the highest levels, barely entering R.E.M. and the deep restorative levels that bring rest and healing to the body. It's not the typical insomnia, that keeps one awake and pacing the floor. I would prefer that. I could at least work or clean. I have no problem falling asleep, but when I wake up it's as if I never slept at all."

"Goodness. Do they know what's causing it?"

I leaned back into the couch. "The primary care physician tried to label me with Fibromyalgia, but I explained to him that I toss and turn all night, and that's what's causing my aches and pains, not the other way around.

He agreed, "It's not Fibromyalgia."

"That makes sense." She jotted a note.

"Since none of the medications helped me get anymore sleep. I'm down to it being all in my head." I took a slow, deep breath to calm myself. "I wouldn't be here at all, except that you used to go to church with my friends and you have a great reputation. No one wants to find out they're crazy, right?" A nervous laugh escaped.

Shelly joined me in laughing. "Tell me what's going on in your life these days."

I told her about my bookkeeping job and how I wanted to be a full-time writer. "It's tough doing both."

"I'm sure it is. What else is going on?" Shelly scratched at her note pad again.

I grabbed a piece of chocolate to buy time while I contemplated how much to share. "Well," I squirreled the candy in my cheek, "two decades ago I received a promise from God for a husband and I'm drying on the vine while I wait for it to come to fruition."

Shelley shifted straight in her chair. "That's a big deal."

"It is, especially when you consider that being married is the only thing I've wanted all these years. And I thank God that I can't hear my clock ticking. I've long ago reconciled myself to the fact that children aren't in my future. Whatever happens, happens."

We continued to discuss the past few decades. I shared with her how I'd received my bachelor's degree, been involved in different singles, youth and college ministries, and finally my financial services ministry and the failed attempts to make that my new career.

She made a few more notes, then leaned forward. "I want you to hear me. I'm not saying you need to leave your church, but find a Bible study or another group in a larger church."

My eyes widened, "I don't think I could do another group for singles. I'd now be the older lady—the one the young ones feel sorry for."

"It doesn't have to be for singles. You can do anything with Christian women in it. They'll have brothers, neighbors, nephews, and uncles. Go where there are more people, which means more opportunities for God to move. Enlarge your circles."

"I've already done tons of activities where I could've met men, but I'll do what you suggest. You're the professional."

I'd met with her every other week for a couple of months when I reported that I'd joined a friend at another church.

Her face lit up. "Did you see anyone you like?"

For the life of me I could not figure out why she'd ask me so quickly. Don't these things take time? "Yes."

"Tell me about him."

I told her that he was in my line-of-sight to the pastor. "He didn't have a wedding band, but he was with an older woman. Could be his wife; you never know these days. Look at George and Barbara Bush. She looked like his mother until recently."

"Then your homework this week is to ask the pastor about him. He should know his flock."

I'd already met the pastor at a meet-and-greet the previous weekend and explained how I'd come to his church. That Sunday I went up to him after service and asked him about the man I'd spotted.

I pointed him out with my eyes and a nod. "In the red shirt over there."

"Ah, Dean Friscea. He's another single never-been-married like you. Go introduce yourself."

I stood there dumbfounded. Was he out of his mind? Shouldn't I take a year or so to contemplate it?

Before I could talk myself out of it, I decided I'd take his advice as a "thus sayeth the Lord." By the time I returned to my pew to retrieve my purse, the man was standing in my way. There was no getting out of it.

I reached my hand out, feeling like a dork. "Hello, my name is Sally Hampton and I'm new."

He smiled and met my hand. "I'm Dean and this is my mother Jean."

"Nice to meet you." I said to both of them.

His mother said, "It's the first Sunday and they have coffee and donuts in the fellowship hall. Would you like to join us?"

I did join them and sat chit-chatting with Jean while Dean made his way around the room. A real social butterfly.

They invited me to lunch with them after church services for the next five months, until finally he asked me out on a date.

We dated for a year and he proposed.

We both married for the first time at the age of fifty, and I still have the sleep problem. I consider it my blessing in disguise.

Sally Friscea, an Army Brat, served four years herself. Since then she's been a bookkeeper, received a degree in Legal Studies and a teaching certification in Home Economics. She is a multi-genre award winning author and member of Word Weavers International. She writes novels, shorter fiction and maintains a blog.

A Time to Cast Away Stones

Michael L. Anderson

My tie was too tight and I forgot my belt. My hand smelled like Vitalis from smoothing my cowlick. The air conditioner was "on the blink" again, and I wiped away eyelid perspiration with a torn worn tissue. Nausea wrestled with me as I tried to find fresh air through the pungent perfume radiating from the lady sitting behind me. In the summer of '65, I disliked church even more than Sunday school.

I didn't want to be here, but it beat being home. Pew bound and always sitting upfront in the second row, organ side, I was wedged between members of the DeHaven family. I couldn't see my friends sitting together in the back row, but I could hear their spontaneous giggle eruptions that gleaned dirty looks from grumpy grownups.

Reverend Siefert, a stout bald minister, began the service requesting the congregation stand to sing the doxology. *Stand? You've got to be kidding. We barely squeezed into this pew only moments earlier.* Thankfully, it was a short song and we sat again, wrestling for ample bum space. I hated church.

The next thirty minutes would torment me as I anticipated another boring sermon. The pastor would parade up and down the platform the stage bellowing about God this and Satan that. Some in the congregation probably liked his wailing voice, but to my teen ears, his words resembled those of a muffled Peanuts cartoon … wah-wah-wah. In my eyes, Reverend Siefert resembled a geezer

Charlie Brown with a scoop of the Pillsbury Doughboy mixed in.

Why was I sitting in a pew with our neighbors and not with my own family? My parents never attended church for reasons unknown to me. Conversely, the DeHavens, attended church eight days a week. They offered to pick me up and bring me home in their family vehicle for every church service, and my parents agreed. It was fine by me too because meant not being around my step-dad.

My home was not a happy one. I was the extra baggage my step-dad took on when he married my mom several years earlier. My mother wanted *this* marriage to succeed so she did anything to ensure this husband felt like a king. To me, he was no kind king, but a ruthless emperor and I was the lowly serf. I felt intimidated and unloved when he was around, so a weekly ride in a church-bound car with the DeHavens became a welcomed refuge for me.

While I didn't care for Sunday school, at least, I mixed with other teens. We could talk about baseball, music, or the latest movies. And when the teacher finally forced us to listen to the lesson, we could still sneak glances out the window or daydream. But after class, attending the church service was like eating broccoli after banana pudding.

This Sunday's service, I was *totally* bored. I removed a hymnal from the back of the pew and began perusing the first few pages. I quietly reasoned at the top of each page, stood the hymn's title along with the name of the person who wrote it. I desperately created a new game to pass the sermon time. My game's object? Find which hymn writer had the shortest name and which one had the longest.

Soon after I began playing, I ran across a hymn that didn't have an author. Instead it read "public domain" in the place where the author's name should be. *What? Nobody wrote it?* I became curious at this hymn and examined the lyrics.

Wait just a second! This was no hymn.
I'd heard this hymn on the radio—on a pop-hits station. The song was titled Turn, Turn, Turn—same title as the hymnal page— and sung by a band called the Byrds. I couldn't believe my eyes. One of my favorite songs was actually a hymn? But there it was...right smack dab in the first few pages of a worn church hymnal.

What could it mean? Did God place this particular hymn into my pew game to help me pass the time in church...or for some other reason?

I slowly read each word of Turn, Turn, Turn, again, again, and again, trying hard to understand them. "A time to keep, and a time to cast away... a time to rend, and a time to sew ... a time to keep silence, and a time to speak ..."

Reading the footnotes on the page, I learned the lyrics actually came from the Bible. The words were not penned by the Byrds, but written by Solomon in the Book of Ecclesiastes way back when. I momentarily swapped the hymnal for my Bible and looked up the Scriptures, totally oblivious to the sermon still dragging on. I thought about my situation at home, and realized the words of this hymn— or pop song—were timeless, and as applicable in today's world as they were in Solomon's time.

Could it be God wanted me to find these words today? Was He providing me some clarity in understanding my rotten home life? Was He encouraging me to endure a little longer?

From that day forward, church became meaningful ... spiritual. I began reading my Bible regularly. I internalized those words from Ecclesiastes and they empowered me when nothing else did during that season of my youth. Those living lyrics instilled in me a creed to live by and helped me get through the remaining turbulent days of high school. My home situation didn't seem so forever anymore.

The DeHavens were faithful servants in taking a younger me to church every week for years. I am forever grateful for them. Seeds were planted in the heart of a teenager those Sundays that eventually took root and brought forth good fruit.

"To everything there is a season, and a time to every purpose under the heaven."

Michael is a freelance contributing writer and product reviewer for various publications. His *Writing for Magazines* workshop is popular at writers conferences. He is an active member of Word Weavers International and Co-Founder of the Christian Authors Guild.

An Accidental Blessing

Kathy Keenum

There was a young man named Marco. He was a tall athletic man admired by women. But, he was on a destructive path. Marco was well known for fighting, drinking and getting into trouble. Marco's mother died in a car accident when he was 7 years old. The accident left Marco with stitches and some broken bones, but he survived. After the accident, his father had thrown himself into work. This left Marco often alone. Grief and anger built up over time and he became known for intimidating and bullying people.

One Friday night during a drag race he lost control of his car, rolled it several times and crashed. After the paramedics cut him out of the car, Marco was transported to the hospital. The ER doctors were very concerned. He had head and spinal injuries along with other fractures and internal bleeding. He was taken into surgery, but was not given much of a chance at survival. His family braced for the news that he had passed during the surgery.

Miraculously, Marco made it through the surgery and lived through the night. He was in a coma for several days but eventually woke. He recovered from the surgery that repaired his abdominal bleeding. However, he was paralyzed from the waist down and the brain injury caused other problems. He had to learn to talk again and regain the coordination in his hands and arms. He spent several months in a rehab facility to learn how to do things in a wheel chair and retrain his brain.

It was at the rehab facility that he learned about the Lord and gave his life to Christ. He met an older man named Samuel, who was recovering from a stroke. He also met and married Sarah, the love of his life.

Many years later he was telling his story to a group of teenagers. He was working as a mentor helping kids at risk. One of the boys asked "Do you ever wish you hadn't gone drag racing that night so that you wouldn't be paralyzed now?" He shocked the group when he replied "No. If I had never had the accident, I would never have found the Lord, I would never have met and married my wife and I would probably be dead by now."

The boy continued, "Did you ever get mad at God for being paralyzed?" Marco replied, "At first I was angry and bitter, and blamed God. But Samuel had given me a Bible. He explained that Jesus Christ was God's son and Jesus died to pay the price for all the wrong things I had ever done. Then Jesus rose from the grave and went back to Heaven. Samuel said Jesus is our savior and we need to believe and have a personal relationship with God.

Samuel quoted Romans 10: 9 "If you declare with your mouth, "Jesus is Lord," and believe in your heart that God raised him from the dead, you will be saved." It took a while for me to understand. My background had left me suspicious and untrusting. But little by little I began to understand and I believed. After I gave my life to the Lord, the anger and bitterness was gone."

Marco added, "I didn't know it at the time, but that accident was the best blessing the Lord could have ever given me. It changed the path I was on. It saved my life. Let me share a verse that I try to live by; Ephesians 4:2-3, "Be completely humble and gentle; be patient, bearing with one another in love. Make every effort to keep the unity of the Spirit through the bond of peace."

Kathy Keenum is an innovative writer with a desire for the Lord. As a Christian, she has written poems and stories centered on the Lord. Her path has taken her through many careers. Now, writing is her passion.

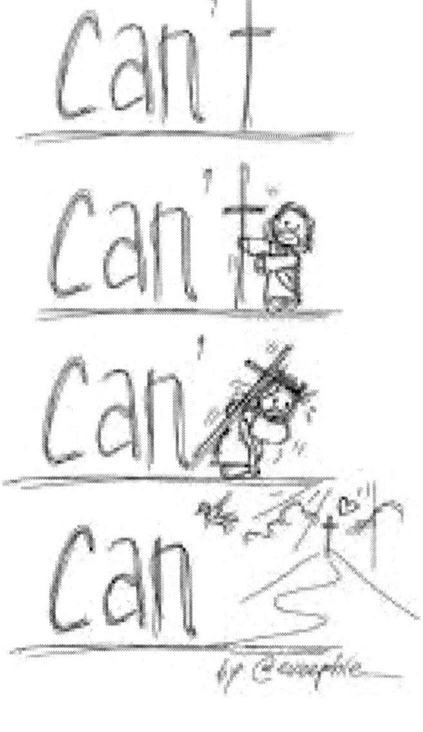
Can't
Can't
Can'
Can

Croaker

John Leatherman

For years, the nicest thing my big brother had ever done for me was to put a frog in my hand when I was six.

It happened on a day when I hadn't done much to deserve niceness from Robert. First I screamed and cried to Mom until she forced him take me frogging with him and his buddies, Brett and Mark.

Then I got the wagon with all the frog buckets stuck in the mud on the way to the pond. Next, at the shore, I tried to get a frog and only got really wet, falling into the water and scaring away two big bullfrogs he was about to catch.

Finally, on the way back, I got the wagon stuck again in the same mud. While pulling it out, I spilled Robert's bucket of frogs. In the ensuing recovery scramble, Brett and Mark claimed Robert's best spring peepers—having already snagged those bullfrogs Robert would have caught at the pond if not for me.

Back home, the three friends hashed out the rules for a frog-jumping contest. Should they measure to the back leg or the nose? Whose feet would they use to measure the jumps? And did the winner *get* something, or did the loser have to *do* something?

Dripping and dejected, without even a little bitty tree toad of my own to enter in the contest, I sulked in the sandbox. The last part of the conversation I remember was Mark proposing the loser would have to take me frogging every week for the rest of the summer.

Then Robert came up to me and said, "Listen, David, I feel bad that you didn't catch any frogs today. Why don't you take this one?"

I looked up. He held out an actual frog! For me!

"Thanks, Robert!" I cupped my hands, and he gave it to me. It felt cool and slimy. "Can I call him Speedy?"

"Whatever you want, Dear Brother." He grinned. "He's yours."

I set Speedy down on the patio, basking in the words. *Dear Brother*. After everything I'd done, he was still my loving brother.

I leapt out of the sandbox and ran to the house for a jar with air holes. But my foot hit something that felt a little too soft to be patio, and a little too hard to be a weed.

I looked down to see a gooey glob under my shoe, something like a mixture of mayonnaise and jelly. Only with legs.

I fell down and cried. How could I do that? I'd squashed Speedy! The only nice thing Robert ever did for me, and I ruined it!

For about five years, I believed that. I didn't want to go near a frog again, afraid I might kill it. But I had a big brother who loved me and watched out for me. The tradeoff was worth it.

Then our big sister, Amy, told us about dissecting a frog in high school biology. I realized I'd have to do that someday and accepted it with rationalization. "I'd be okay with that. I mean, that frog is already dead, so I can't kill it. It won't be another Speedy."

Thirteen-year-old Robert laughed. "David, are you still hung up over that? You didn't kill Speedy!"

"But I stepped on him."

"Yeah, and did you ever wonder why, as you lit off running, he didn't so much as hop an inch? Brett found him at the bottom of his bucket, *suffocated* under five layers of bullfrogs. We gave you a *dead* frog. As a *joke!*"

I stared at Robert in disbelief.

Shrugging, he flashed me a slick smile. "Sorry."

Mom and Amy scowled at each other, agreeing this was "typical Robert."

They took it worse than I did. I thought about it for a while, said, "Huh," and then went to see what was on TV.

Five years of mistaken belief now stood corrected. I wasn't a frog murderer after all! And okay, my brother had been a jerk, but at least he loved me enough to tell the truth.

A dead frog had kept a bad day from becoming a horrible day. That really was a blessing in disguise.

John Leatherman is a writer, cartoonist, and editor. He has written book reviews for *Christian Retailing* and word games for International Puzzle Syndicate. A longtime member and former officer of Word Weavers International, he has won multiple awards from the Florida-Georgia chapter's annual Tapestry contest.

Oh, and in the daytime, he's a software engineer with two kids.

My Basket Overflows

Carolyn Fisher

My basket overflows with blessings big and small.

There are almost too many to try and count them all.

I want Jesus to get the credit for all that He has done.

So, I try to name them daily; each, and every one

When I close my eyes at night and think about the day.

I know His hand was in it, in some small, special way.

He has led me to the path where He wants me to go.

He said, "Don't try to run ahead of me, just go slow."

I must learn to listen closely when He talks to me.

His Word is always special; He speaks to all, you see.

Try to count your blessings daily; listen and try to hear.

He always has a word; something you might share

He loves us so, and truly wants to bless us each day.

But, we must draw close to Him; He is the only way.

While dying, my husband asked me to write a book on how God healed our marriage. It was released the month after his death. Journaling the next year inspired me to write another book which I hope to publish, "*My Bucket Overflows.*" This poem is at the beginning of the book.

There Shall be Showers of Blessings

Daniel Webster Whittle (1840-1901)

There shall be showers of blessing:
This is the promise of love;
There shall be seasons refreshing,
Sent from the Savior above.

Refrain:

Showers of blessing,
Showers of blessing we need:
Mercy-drops round us are falling,
But for the showers we plead.

There shall be showers of blessing,
Precious reviving again;
Over the hills and the valleys,
Sound of abundance of rain.

There shall be showers of blessing;
Send them upon us, O Lord;
Grant to us now a refreshing,
Come, and now honor Thy Word.

There shall be showers of blessing:
Oh, that today they might fall,
Now as to God we're confessing,
Now as on Jesus we call!

There shall be showers of blessing,
If we but trust and obey;
There shall be seasons refreshing,
If we let God have His way.

Blessed by Design

Nanette Gordon

The woman arrived at the new church with a dose of enthusiasm and a dash of skepticism. During her search for a place of worship, she had attended Sunday morning services at various churches and had witnessed scary places, sparse spaces and blank faces. She observed experimental faiths, lack of Bible Scripture references. She endured loud worship bands, along with dancing, smoke and light shows.

She was disappointed, yet not discouraged. She frequently prayed about her mission to find a suitable church and was peaceful. She felt moved by the Spirit that she was on the right path, to the right place and it would become apparent at the right time. She was encouraged that it would be a worthwhile journey.

The woman searched her city and neighboring communities. She reviewed their websites to learn about their doctrine. Since she previously attended a large church, she was being lead to find a traditional church setting with strong evangelical and Bible based values. After attending at several locations, she found a quaint church about three miles from her home. Her research determined that it closely matched her doctrinal beliefs. She attended a few Sunday services and she was pleased with the pastor's sermons.

She carefully observed the handling of church rituals and format, such as collection of offerings, doxology and benediction. Deacons and elders were in formal attire. The sanctuary had a classic and reverent atmosphere, with wooden pews, Bibles and offering envelopes. She became a member that October.

As a naturally outgoing person, she volunteered to be a greeter for the Christmas pageant. It was during that weekend she was invited to a brunch at the home of an elder. She was introduced to church members. She noticed a distinguished looking man walk in that she had seen at services. They exchanged greetings but never had an opportunity to talk. She spent most of her time chatting with a cheerful woman. The handsome stranger looked over at her several times that afternoon, even staring at times. She felt flattered yet uneasy. She did not know anything about him. After brunch, she left to greet at the Christmas presentation.

By January, the woman became interested in fellowship, women's ministry Bible study and continuing education. The subject in Sunday school was The Book of Revelation. She was excited about this class, since she never studied it in depth before. During her first visit, she met the teacher who was one of the elders, along with the nice looking, blue eyed man she met at the brunch.

She enjoyed Sunday school class and the lively discussions. The man she had met also attended each week. She observed that he always arrived and left church alone. He was always greeting people, both familiar faces and new visitors. She learned later learned that he was an elder and a widower.

After a while, the woman was asked if she would be interested in helping manage the greeters, welcome and hospitality team. She was honored and replied that she would consider it. She received a personal invitation by telephone from the pastor, who also wanted her help with event planning. She accepted this call to ministry, which she had been praying about.

The greeter position lead her to grow closer to her new friend. As an elder, he was always at the rear of the sanctuary and nearby. They chatted weekly in the welcome center.

That summer, she invited church friends, as well as the gentleman, to a Fourth of July party at her home. It was a great time and she felt she had a special connection with this man. She began to invite him to movies and other socials, even though he did not reciprocate by calling her and inviting her to date. They went out several months as friends.

In late summer, they were having dinner together. During their conversation he informed her that he was leaving this church. She was stunned and devastated. She asked him why but he replied that he would not reveal the private reason.

They further discussed their relationship. He asked her why she had decided to ask him out for movies and various occasions, even though he didn't initiate contact himself. She explained she thought he might be shy, and that she enjoyed his company and liked planning social outings, which was natural for her. She told him she had fond feelings towards him and thought he felt the same. He explained that he had not dated anyone since his wife died and didn't think he ever would again. He said he was surprised that he enjoyed her attention and easily accepted her invitations. But she felt heartbroken. She didn't know if they would continue to see each other after he left, and she decided to leave her ministry and this church. Several people knew about their relationship, and she felt awkward.

Soon after this, they attended a fund raising dinner banquet she had prearranged. However, she thought she would never see him again after that evening. She didn't know what God could be telling her through all of this. But she trusted His sovereign wisdom and prayed he would reveal His plan.

After a few weeks, the couple discovered they enjoyed their companionship. There was chemistry and compatibility. They prayed about it and are now dating, spending most weekends, church services and small groups together. They are placing God in first place, guarding their hearts and purity.

It was a blessing in disguise. Although their time at that church ended, a close friendship blossomed in its place. At first, it seemed tragic that their ministries at this church were short lived, but God's perfect plan and purpose shined through. Their initial feelings of pain, loss and disappointment were replaced with a new season of hopeful expectancy for a bright future.

Nanette Gordon grew up in the city and suburbs of New York. She displayed her creative talents early with poetry and essays. Her studies excelled in literature, history and art. Nanette has enjoyed success working in journalism, advertising, marketing, event planning and publicity.

Living Parables of Central Florida

Living Parables of Central Florida, Inc., of which EABooks Publishing is a division, supports Christian charities providing for the needs of their communities and are encouraged to join hands and hearts with like-minded charities to better meet unmet needs in their communities. Annually the Board of Directors chooses the recipients of seed money to facilitate the beginning stages of these charitable activities.

Mission Statement

To empower start up, nonprofit organizations financially, spiritually, and with sound business knowledge to participate successfully as a responsible 501(c)3 organization that contributes to the Kingdom work of God.

Incubator Program

The goal of the Incubator Program: The Small Non-Profit Success Incubator Program, provides a solid foundation for running a successful non-profit through a year-long coaching process, eventually allowing these charities to successfully apply for grants and loans from others so they can further meet unmet needs in their communities.

Living Parables of Central Florida, a 501c3

Made in the USA
Columbia, SC
26 April 2021